I0519779

THIS BOOK BELONGS TO

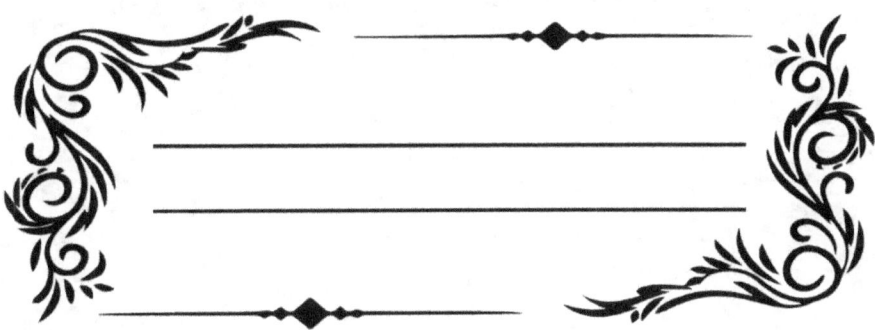

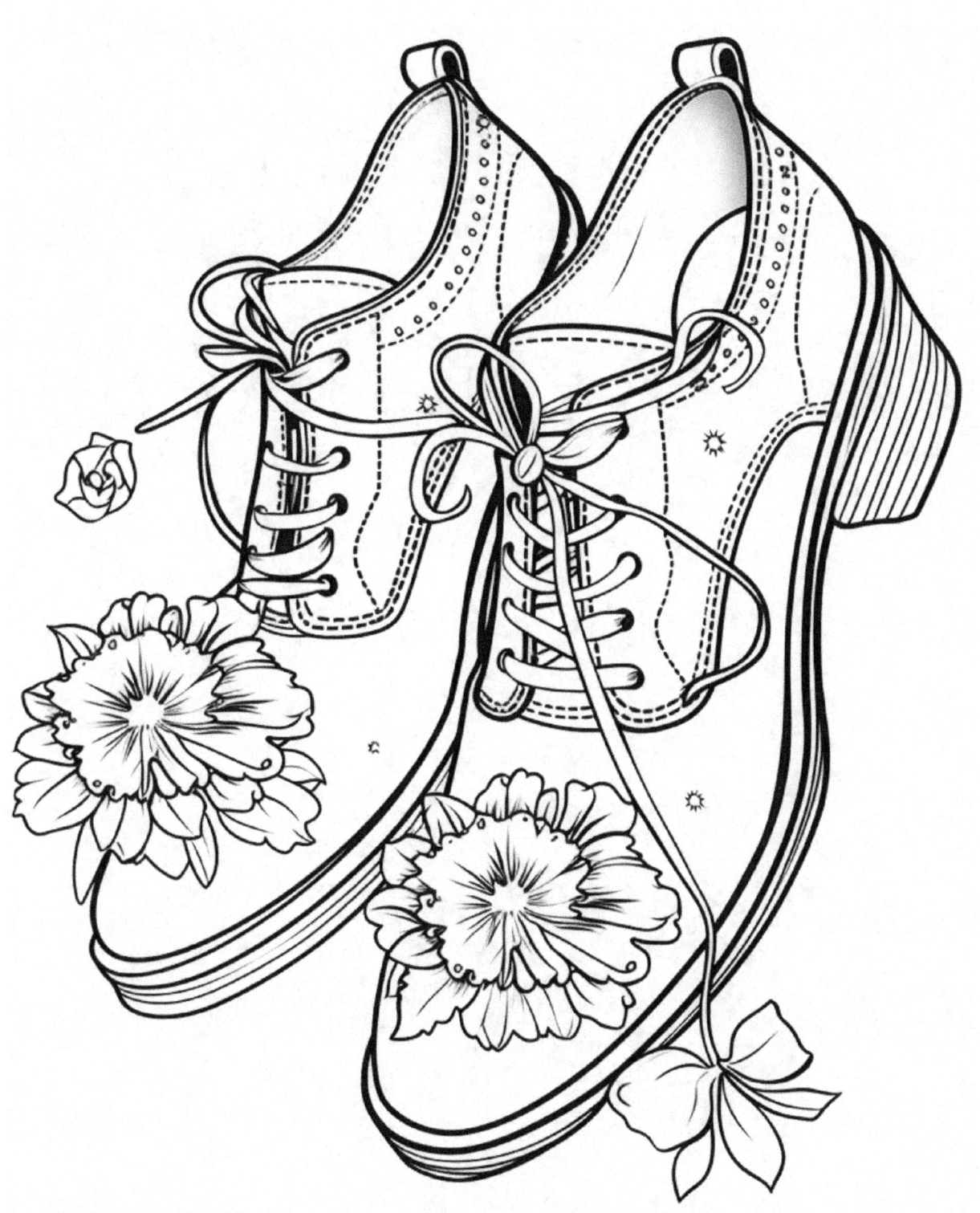

Thank You!

As the author of this gratitude journal, I wanted to take a moment to express our heartfelt gratitude for choosing our book and completing this incredible journey. It brings us great joy to know that our small, family-owned company has been a part of your life.

At our company, we pour our hearts and souls into creating quality children's books that inspire and empower young minds, just like you.

If you enjoyed this journal and found it to be a source of joy, encouragement, and growth, we kindly invite you to leave a review on Amazon. Your words carry immense power and can make a significant impact on our small business. Your support will not only help us reach more children but also inspire us to continue creating meaningful books.

We understand that leaving a review may seem like a small action, but to us, it means the world. Your support will enable us to continue producing quality books that touch the lives of young readers and nourish their imaginations.

This Is Our Family

Stela Stere

Cucus Surus

Tande Mande

 # Contact us!

It is important for us to let you know that we appreciate any feedback
on our creations and if you have any suggestions for improvement,
you can contact us at our email address:

gopublishforyou@gmail.com

Are you following us on Instagram?

If not, down below you can find the link to our Instagram page, where
you can see other creations we have made, announcements about our
books or announcements about our new releases.

https://www.instagram.com/cristiartdesign/

www.ingramcontent.com/pod-product-compliance
Lightning Source LLC
Chambersburg PA
CBHW081005120626
46546CB00010B/3014